EXPLORE SPACE!

EXPLORE THE SUN

BY EMMA HUDDLESTON

CONTENT CONSULTANT
DEBRA ELMEGREEN, PhD
PROFESSOR OF ASTRONOMY
VASSAR COLLEGE

Kids Core
An Imprint of Abdo Publishing
abdobooks.com

abdobooks.com

Printed in the United States of America, North Mankato, Minnesota
052021
092021

 THIS BOOK CONTAINS RECYCLED MATERIALS

Cover Photo: Goddard/GSFC/SDO/NASA
Interior Photos: iStockphoto, 4–5, 9, 10, 23, 25; Goddard/GSFC/SDO/NASA, 6, 15; SOFIA/Lim, De Buizer, & Radomski et al./ESA/Herschel/JPL-Caltech/NASA, 12–13; Goddarc/ESA/NASA, 14; Mark Garlick/Science Source, 16; Shutterstock Images, 18, 22, 29; Chris Butler/Science Source, 20–21; Avigator Photographer/iStockphoto, 26

Editor: Marie Pearson
Series Designer: Katharine Hale

Library of Congress Control Number: 2020948354

Publisher's Cataloging-in-Publication Data

Names: Huddleston, Emma, author.
Title: Explore the sun / by Emma Huddleston
Description: Minneapolis, Minnesota : Abdo Publishing, 2022 | Series: Explore space! | Includes online resources and index.
Identifiers: ISBN 9781532195419 (lib. bdg.) | ISBN 9781644945452 (pbk.) | ISBN 9781098215729 (ebook)
Subjects: LCSH: Outer space--Exploration--Juvenile literature. | Sun--Juvenile literature. | Stars--Juvenile literature. | Solar system--Juvenile literature. | Astronomy--Juveni e literature.
Classification: DDC 523.7--dc23

CONTENTS

The Sun gives off light, which heats nearby planets.

CHAPTER 1

BRIGHT STAR

The Sun is a star. It is a ball of hot gas. Temperatures in parts reach higher than 3 million degrees Fahrenheit (1.7 million°C). The Sun shines brightly. Its light spreads out into space. The light hits objects, such as planets. It warms them up.

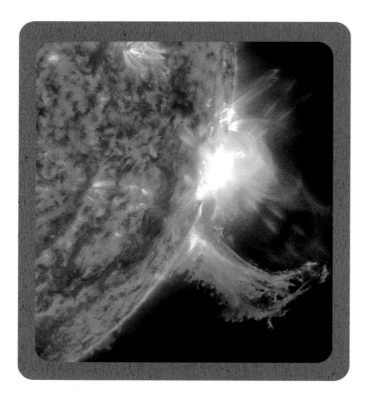

A solar flare, *top*, is a flash of bright light on the surface of the Sun. A prominence, *bottom*, is gas that extends from the Sun.

Hot gas rises to the Sun's surface. It bubbles up, cools, and then falls back down. Sometimes cool gas gets trapped at the surface. It cannot fall back down. These cooler areas look like dark spots on the Sun's surface. They are called sunspots. After a time, they disappear again. Near sunspots, **solar** flares occur. A solar flare is a bright burst of energy. It may glow for a few minutes or hours.

At the Center

The Sun is at the center of our solar system. A solar system is made up of a star and all the planets and other space bodies that **orbit** the star. Our solar system has eight planets. Earth is the third planet from the Sun. Our solar system has more than 190 moons.

Spinning Around

The Sun spins in place. Since it is not solid, it does not spin at the same rate in every area. The equator, or middle region, of the Sun **rotates** once in about 25 Earth days. Areas near the top and bottom of the Sun take about 36 days to rotate.

The Sun is 864,000 miles (1.4 million km) wide. It's made mostly of burning hydrogen gas. It does not have a solid surface. The core is at the Sun's center. It is the hottest part of the Sun at 27 million degrees Fahrenheit (15 million°C). Temperatures are cooler outside the core.

The surface of the Sun that people can see is called the photosphere. It reaches about 10,000 degrees Fahrenheit (5,500°C). Above this is a layer of gas called the chromosphere. Here the temperature rises. The highest layer is the corona. This layer is even hotter. Temperatures here reach higher than 3 million degrees Fahrenheit (1.7 million°C). The corona spreads millions of miles into space.

The Sun is very bright even from Earth.

Plants could not grow without the Sun.

The Sun is a special star because it is the closest to Earth. Its energy gives Earth light and heat. Without it, life would not be possible.

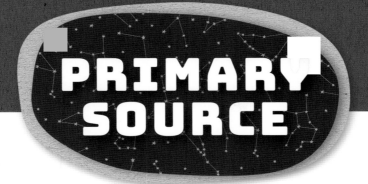

In 2020, NASA sent a vehicle called the Solar Orbiter to study the Sun. It took detailed pictures of the Sun. NASA explained the importance of the mission:

> We've studied the Sun for decades, but there is still more to learn about the center of our solar system.

Source: "NASA Scientist Talks about Upcoming Mission to Sun." *KLTV*, 7 Feb. 2020, kltv.com. Accessed 24 July 2020.

What's the Big Idea?

Read this quote carefully. What is its main idea?

Stars form in clouds of dust and gas.

CHAPTER 2

HOT BALL OF GAS

Scientists believe the Sun began forming 4.6 billion years ago. Its life began in a protosolar nebula, which is a giant, spinning cloud of gas and dust. Scientists think that these particles from the cloud began clumping together.

A protostar, such as the one in the center of this image glowing behind a cloud, takes many millions of years to become a star like the Sun.

The clump grew for millions of years. The core got hotter and more packed together. It became a protostar. The protostar kept pulling in more gas.

Eventually, the protostar reached 18 million degrees Fahrenheit (10 million°C). It was hot

The Sun will continue to give off light for billions of years.

enough for nuclear fusion. Nuclear fusion is when **nuclei** join together. The core of the protostar was made mostly of hydrogen gas. When nuclei of this hydrogen fused together, they formed helium gas.

Red giants are old stars that no longer fuse hydrogen in their cores.

When nuclear fusion began, the Sun became a main sequence star. That is the stage of life it is currently in. In this stage, the Sun does not gain mass. It gives off energy. The Sun has been a main sequence star for 4.5 billion years. Scientists believe it will burn for a total of 10 billion years.

End of Life

All stars die at some point. When the Sun can no longer fuse hydrogen in its core, the outer layers will expand. The Sun will look red because it will be cooler. The core will **collapse** and heat up. It will fuse helium to carbon. The Sun may grow 100 times bigger. This is the red giant stage. When the Sun is a red giant, it may swell so big that it reaches the planet Mars.

How Big Is the Sun?

The Sun is a medium-sized star. Some stars are ten times smaller than the Sun. Others are more than 1,000 times the size of the Sun. But the Sun is much larger than the planets that orbit it. It would take about 1.3 million Earths to fill the Sun.

Life Cycle of the Sun

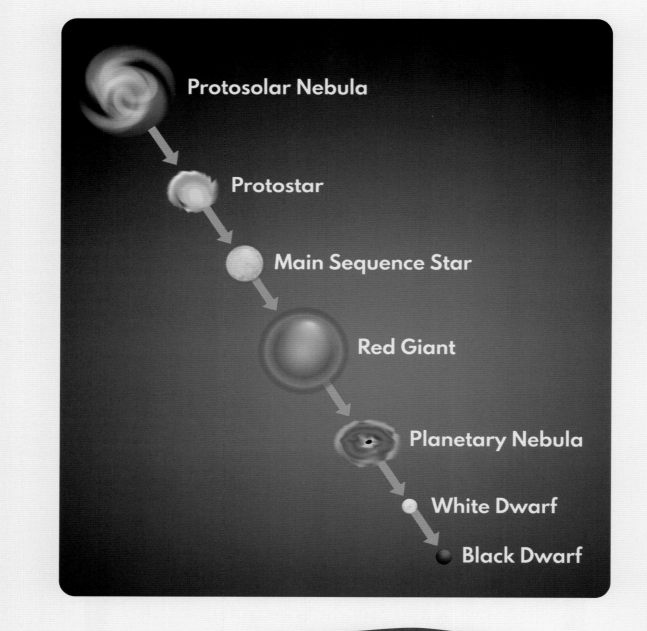

The Sun and other stars of similar size have several life cycle stages.

When all the helium in the core is fused into carbon, fusion stops. The outer layers will separate from the core. They will form a planetary nebula and spread into space. At this stage, the core is known as a white dwarf. Eventually, it will cool completely and become a black dwarf.

Explore Online

Visit the website below. Does it give any new information about how stars form that wasn't in Chapter Two?

Stars and Galaxies

abdocorelibrary.com/explore-the-sun

The Sun is one of billions of stars in the Milky Way Galaxy, shown in this illustration.

CHAPTER 3

AFFECTING LIFE ON EARTH

The Sun is constantly moving. It orbits the center of the Milky Way galaxy once every 230 million years. A galaxy is a collection of solar systems. It also includes gas and dust that can make new stars.

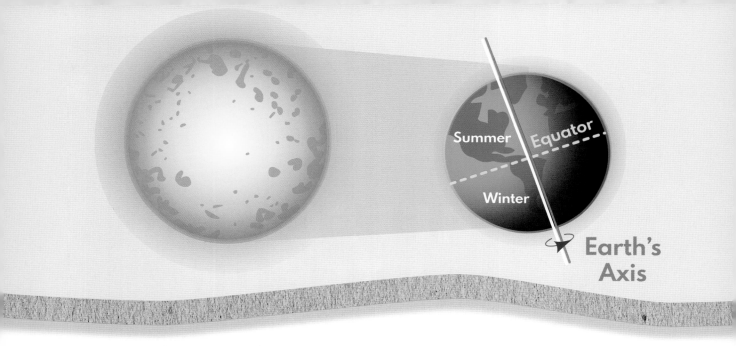

Summer

Equator

Winter

Earth's Axis

The angle of Earth's tilt toward the Sun causes the seasons.

The Sun and Earth each spin on an axis. An axis is an imaginary line through the middle of an object from top to bottom. Earth has a tilted axis. The tilt causes seasons. The Sun's light warms the planets around it. This helps living things on Earth survive. The area of Earth that is tilted toward the Sun gets more direct sunlight. This causes summer. Less direct sunlight causes winter.

A region experiences winter when it is tilted away from the Sun.

A Source of Power

The weather on Earth depends on the Sun. It heats up the air. Air moves based on temperature. Hot air rises. Cool air rushes in to fill space where the warm air was. This process makes breezes and winds.

The Sun also heats up parts of the ocean. Warm water rises. Cool water flows in to replace the warm water. This creates currents. Water and air both move from cool places to warm places.

Auroras

Auroras are light shows caused by the solar wind. The solar wind is made up of **charged** particles that travel from the Sun to Earth. When the particles reach Earth, they hit Earth's air and give off light. The light can be different colors based on the types of gases in the air. Oxygen causes red and yellow. Nitrogen causes red, blue, and violet.

The Sun warms the surface of the ocean.

Solar panels use sunlight to create electricity.

People can capture the Sun's light with solar panels. A solar panel is technology that takes in sunlight and turns it into electricity. Electricity is used to power many things, including homes.

The Sun sends light into space. It warms Earth and makes the planet suitable for life. It will keep burning for billions of years.

Further Evidence

Look at the website below. Does it give any new evidence about orbits to support Chapter Three?

The Sun: Orbits

abdocorelibrary.com/explore-the-sun

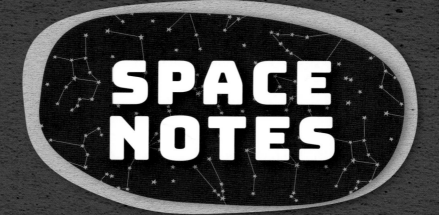

SPACE NOTES

Corona

Chromosphere

Photosphere

Prominence

Core

Sunspot

Solar Flare

Sun Cross Section

Glossary

charged
having a positive or negative electric force

collapse
to cave in on oneself

nuclei
the centers of atoms, which are the building blocks of all matter; matter is any material that takes up space

orbit
to follow an oval-shaped path around a more massive object

rotates
spins or turns around

solar
having to do with the Sun